P9-CML-119

THE LIBRARY OF
CONSTELLATIONS™

The Big Dipper

Stephanie True Peters

The Rosen Publishing Group's
PowerKids Press™
New York

For Dan, who helps me reach the stars

Published in 2003 by The Rosen Publishing Group, Inc.
29 East 21st Street, New York, NY 10010

First Edition

Editor: Jannell Khu
Book Design: Michael Caroleo, Michael Donnellan, Michael de Guzman
Photo Credits: Cover and p. 4 © Roger Ressmeyer/CORBIS; back cover, title page and p.8 © Bode's Uranographia, 1801, courtesy of the Science, Industry & Business Library, the New York Public Library, Astor, Lenox, and Tilden Foundations; pp.6–7 © Stapleton Collection/CORBIS; p.11 (Native American) © Geoffrey Clements/CORBIS; p.12 © Ken Graham/Stone; p.15 © North Wind Pictures; p.16 © NOAO/AURA/NSF; p.17 James A. Sugar/© CORBIS; p.19 (bottom) © David Gubernick/CORBIS; p.19 (top) Michael de Guzman; p.20 © Kennan Ward/CORBIS.

Peters, Stephanie True, 1965–
The big dipper / Stephanie True Peters.
 p. cm. — (Library of constellations)
 Includes bibliographical references and index.
 Summary: Examines the constellation known as the Big Dipper, the stars of which it is composed, and how to locate it in the night sky.
  ISBN 0-8239-6162-1 (library binding)
  1. Ursa Major—Juvenile literature. [1. Ursa Major. 2. Constellations. 3. Stars.] I. Title. II. Series: Peters, Stephanie True, 1965– . Library of constellations.
 QB802 .P414 2003
 523.8—dc21
                                                                                    2001004956

Manufactured in the United States of America

Contents

1   What Is the Big Dipper?   5

2   What People Saw in the Big Dipper   6

3   Greek Legend of the Great Bear   9

4   Native American Legend of the Great Bear   10

5   The Big Dipper's Stars   13

6   Finding the North Star   14

7   Stargazing with Telescopes   17

8   Where to Find the Big Dipper   18

9   The Speed of Light   21

10   Stars on the Move   22

Glossary   23

Index   24

Web Sites   24

What Is the Big Dipper?

Look at the night sky and you can see shapes that look like giant, connect-the-dot drawings. The Big Dipper is one of the easiest star **formations** to find in the night sky. It is made of seven bright stars that form the shape of a bent handle and a bowl. The Big Dipper is not a true constellation, which is a group of stars that has been given a name. It is an **asterism**, a group of stars that is part of a larger constellation.

The Big Dipper is part of a constellation called **Ursa Major**, or the Great Bear. Ursa Major is one of the 88 **official** constellations. Ursa Major is not that easy to see, so most people look for the Big Dipper. Constellations are useful to **astronomers**, scientists who study the sky, and to stargazers. Constellations, and asterisms like the Big Dipper, help break up the big sky into smaller pictures. When you study one picture at a time, the sky does not seem as big.

The Big Dipper gets its name from the long-handled bowls that are used to scoop, or dip up, water.

5

What People Saw in the Big Dipper

Unlike planets, moons, and **comets**, constellations were not discovered. Instead the different shapes and formations of the constellations in the sky were created by people's imaginations. No one knows who first saw the star formation we now call the Big Dipper. What we do know is that many **civilizations** around the world saw its shape and named it. The ancient Greeks saw a bear from the Big Dipper formation. The Chinese described the Big Dipper as a **chariot**. The Romans thought the stars looked like a plow and oxen. The Arabs saw a **coffin** and **mourners** in the sky. The Vikings imagined that the Big Dipper was a wagon that traveled around the sky. In India they believed the stars were seven wise men.

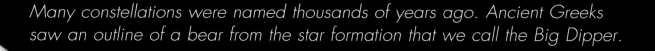
Many constellations were named thousands of years ago. Ancient Greeks saw an outline of a bear from the star formation that we call the Big Dipper.

Greek Legend of the Great Bear

There is an ancient Greek **legend** about the constellation Ursa Major. Zeus, the king of the gods, fell in love with Callisto, a beautiful **nymph** and a hunting **companion** of the goddess Artemis. Callisto gave birth to Zeus's son Arcas. There are different stories as to who turned Callisto into a bear. Some say it was Hera, Zeus's jealous wife. Some stories say it was Artemis. Still other stories say it was Zeus who turned Callisto into a bear to hide her from Hera.

Hunters chased Callisto for years. Even Arcas tried to kill her, because he was not aware that the bear was his mother. Just before Arcas could kill Callisto, Zeus turned her into the constellation we call the Great Bear. The bowl of the Big Dipper is part of the Great Bear's back. The handle is its tail. According to the Greek story, the bear's tail is long because it stretched when Zeus pulled Callisto into the sky!

If you look closely at the Great Bear, you can see the shape of the Big Dipper. The bear's tail is the handle, and the bowl is part of its back.

Native American Legend of the Great Bear

Some Native Americans also have a legend about the Great Bear in the sky. Their legend is used to explain why green leaves turn red in the fall. To these Native Americans, the four stars that form the Big Dipper's bowl look like a bear. The stars that form the handle are three hunters. The bear sleeps in the sky through the winter, the spring, and the summer months. In the fall, the three hunters wake up the bear. Night after night, the hunters chase the bear around the sky and try to kill it with their bows and arrows. When the arrows finally hit the bear, its blood spills down to the earth and onto the tree leaves and stains them red.

Fun Facts

Some Native Americans believed that if a young man could see the double stars in the center of the Big Dipper's handle, he could see well enough to make his mark as a warrior and a hunter!

Instead of the Big Dipper's handle, some Native Americans saw three hunters, like this one, in the star formation.

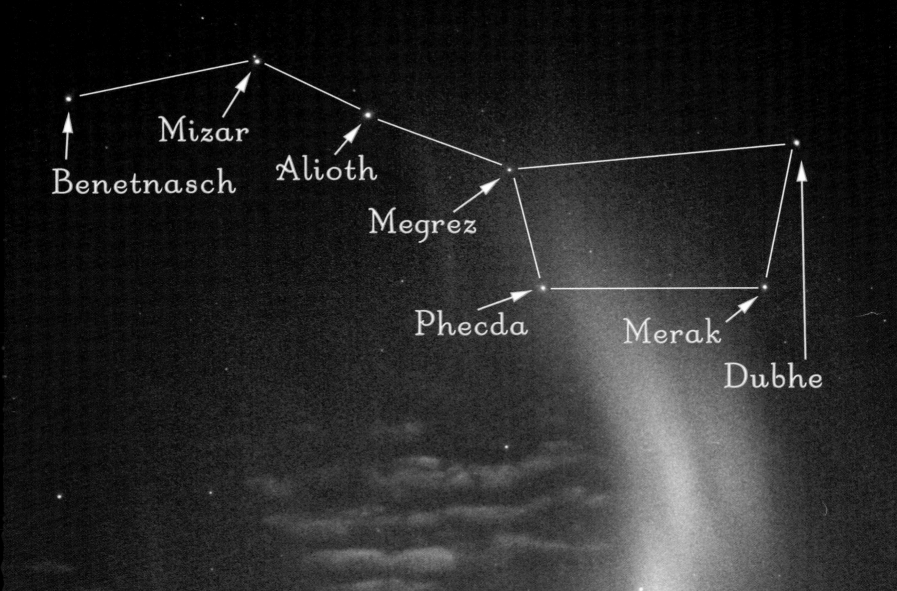

The Big Dipper's Stars

The seven stars of the Big Dipper were named by ancient Arab and Greek stargazers. The three stars that form the handle are named Benetnasch, Mizar, and Alioth. Benetnasch is the end of the handle and means "chief of the mourners." Mizar is the middle star and means "girdle," or "apron." No one knows the meaning of Alioth. The star in the bowl closest to Alioth is Megrez. Megrez means "base of the tail." Below it is Phecda, which means "thigh." Next to Phecda is Merak, or "**loin**." Above Merak is Dubhe, or "bear." Merak and Dubhe also have another name. They're called the Pointer Stars, because a line traced from Merak through Dubhe points to the North Star.

Fun Facts

Around 150 B.C., Greek astronomer Hipparchus ranked the brightness of stars from 1 to 6. Stars ranked 1 were the brightest, and 6 represented the faintest stars.

Most of the stars named from 500 to 2,000 years ago have Arabic names.

Finding the North Star

The North Star, or Polaris, is a very important star. Unlike other stars, it appears to remain fixed in place. If you can find Polaris, you know you are facing north. If you can find the Big Dipper, you can find Polaris. Dubhe and Merak point the way.

Polaris has helped people **navigate** over sea and land for centuries. If you move toward Polaris, you are traveling north. South is behind you. East is to your right. West is to your left. When **slavery** was practiced in the Southern United States, slaves who were escaping knew that if they followed the North Star, they could reach the Northern states and freedom.

Fun Facts

At night, Polaris can help guide you. During the day, the Sun can help you find your direction. The Sun rises in the east and sets in the west.

If you are lost at night, Polaris can help you like a compass. Dubhe and Merak point to Polaris. Once you've spotted Polaris, you know you are facing north.

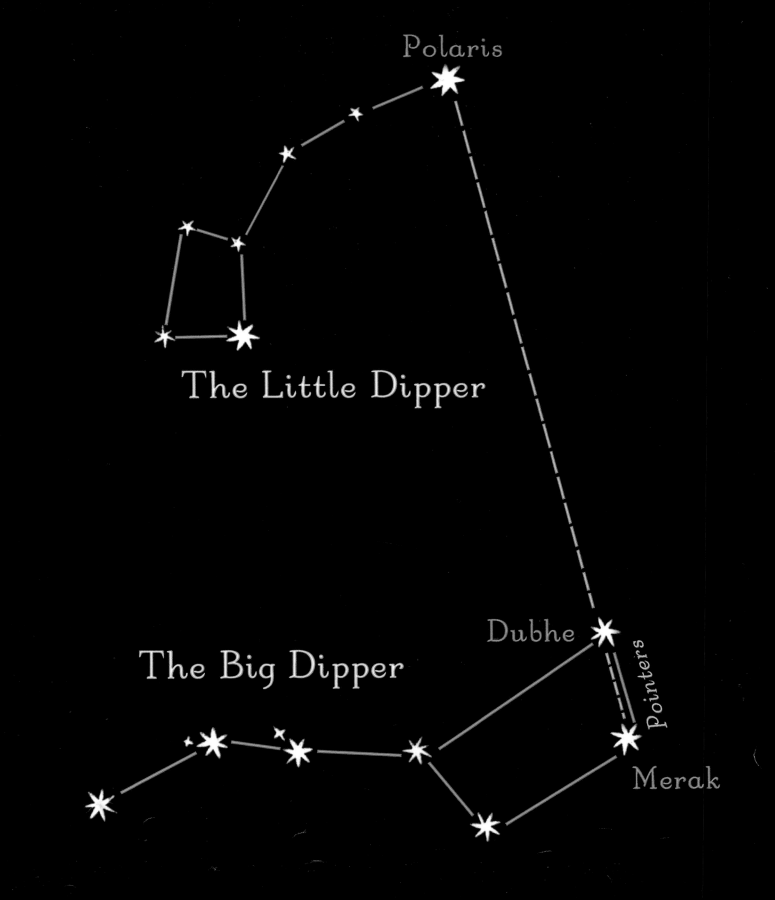

Polaris

The Little Dipper

Dubhe

The Big Dipper

Pointers

Merak

Stargazing with Telescopes

How do astronomers learn about the Big Dipper's stars? They study them through very powerful **telescopes**. A telescope is a scientific instrument. It is made of a tube that **magnifies** objects with lenses and mirrors. Light bounces off an object and passes through a lens at one end of the telescope. You look at the magnified object through an eyepiece at the other end of the telescope. As the light hits a series of mirrors and lenses, it bends, or refracts. As the light refracts, the object is made to appear larger than it actually is. Telescopes can also be used to take pictures of the night sky. Astronomers **photograph** the same part of the sky at different times of the night, or during different seasons. They study the pictures to learn how stars move, how big and bright they are, and what color they are.

Located in Mauna Kea, Hawaii, the Gemini North telescope is one of the largest and most advanced telescopes available to astronomers.

Where to Find the Big Dipper

If you live in the United States or anywhere else in the **Northern Hemisphere**, you should be able to find the Big Dipper at any time of the year. Many star formations disappear below the **horizon**. The horizon is the line where the sky meets the ground, as Earth moves through space. The Big Dipper never disappears, though. It circles Polaris through the four different seasons like a clock hand that moves backward.

The Big Dipper can be seen at a different position on the clock face depending on the season. In the springtime, if you face north, the Big Dipper is straight ahead at twelve o'clock. It is flipped upside down with its bowl pointing west. Summer finds it at nine o'clock, standing on its bowl. In autumn it rests flat and upright at six o'clock. In the winter, the Big Dipper stands on its handle at three o'clock.

The Big Dipper circles Polaris through different seasons.

Winter
9:00 pm

Spring
9:00 pm

Summer
9:00 pm

North Star

Fall
9:00 pm

Benetnasch

635 trillion miles away from Earth
(1,022 trillion km)

Mizar

353 trillion miles away from Earth
(568 trillion km)

The Speed of Light

On a clear night, it seems as though you could reach up and grab the Big Dipper's handle, but that would be impossible. Its stars are very far away from Earth. Astronomers measure the distance to a star in **light-years**. A light-year is the distance light can travel in one year, about 6 **trillion** miles (10 trillion km).

The Big Dipper may look like a flat drawing on the dome of the sky, but not all the seven stars are the same distance from Earth. Of the seven stars that make up the Big Dipper, Mizar is the closest star to Earth. Astronomers figure it is about 353 trillion miles (568 trillion km) away. To reach it, you would have to travel for about 60 years at the speed of light. The farthest star from Earth is Benetnasch. To reach this star, you would have to travel for 108 years at the speed of light. That means Benetnasch is 635 trillion miles (1,022 trillion km) away!

In the Big Dipper's formation, Benetnasch is the farthest star from Earth and Mizar is the closest.

Stars on the Move

Mizar's distance from Benetnasch always changes. This is because stars move, as does everything else in the **universe**. They are so far away from us that they seem to move very, very slowly, but they do move. As the stars in the Big Dipper move, the shape of the Big Dipper changes. The Big Dipper's bowl was smaller and deeper 100,000 years ago. Its handle was nearly straight. Astronomers think the handle will hook down sharply and the bowl will look much flatter 100,000 years from now! For now the Big Dipper looks just like its name, and on a clear, dark night, it is one of the easiest shapes to see in the sky.

Fun Facts

Did you know that the Sun is a star? The Sun is the closest star to Earth. The Sun is 100 times bigger than Earth!

Glossary

asterism (AS-tuh-rih-zem) A group of stars that is a part of a constellation.

astronomers (uh-STRAH-nuh-merz) Scientists who study the Sun, the Moon, the planets, and the stars.

chariot (CHAIR-ee-ut) A two-wheeled carriage pulled by horses.

civilizations (sih-vih-lih-ZAY-shunz) People living in an organized way.

coffin (KAW-fin) A box in which the body of a dead person is buried.

comets (KAH-mits) Heavenly bodies, made up of ice and dust, that look like stars with tails of light.

companion (kum-PAN-yun) A person who often goes along with another.

formations (for-MAY-shunz) The outlines of shapes.

horizon (her-EYE-zun) The line where the sky seems to meet the earth.

legend (LEH-jund) A story passed down that many people believe.

light-years (LYT YEERZ) Units of measurement based on the distance light can travel in one year, 6 trillion miles (10 trillion km).

loin (LOYN) The part of an animal's abdomen between the ribs and the hips.

magnifies (MAG-nih-fyz) Makes something look bigger than it really is.

mourners (MOR-nerz) People who feel sorrow or grief.

navigate (NA-vuh-gayt) To steer on a course during a journey over land or sea.

Northern Hemisphere (NOR-thern HEH-muh-sfeer) The northern half of Earth's surface.

nymph (NIMF) A beautiful female spirit from Greek and Roman mythology.

official (uh-FIH-shul) Having proof that something is formal or legal.

photograph (FOH-tuh-graf) To take a picture with a camera.

slavery (SLAY-vuh-ree) The system of one person "owning" another.

telescopes (TEH-luh-skohps) Instruments used to make distant objects appear closer and larger.

trillion (TRIL-yin) One thousand times one billion; 1,000,000,000,000.

universe (YOO-nih-vers) Everything that exists, including Earth, the planets, the stars, and all of space.

Ursa Major (ER-suh MAY-jer) The constellation near the North Pole that contains the stars that form the Big Dipper.

Index

A
Alioth, 13
Arcas, 9
Artemis, 9
astronomers, 5, 17, 22

B
Benetnasch, 13, 21, 22

C
Callisto, 9
chariot, 6

D
Dubhe, 13, 14

H
Hera, 9

L
light-years, 21

M
Megrez, 13
Merak, 13, 14
Mizar, 13, 21, 22

N
Native Americans, 10
North Star, 13, 14

P
Phecda, 13
planets, 6

T
telescopes, 17

U
Ursa Major, 5, 9

Z
Zeus, 9

Web Sites

To learn more about constellations and the Big Dipper, check out these Web sites:
www.dibonsmith.com
www.lhs.berkeley.edu/starclock